Passenger Poet

Passenger Poet

Audrey Kohler

ISBN 978-1-952872-12-9

Published in the United States by Verge Publishing.
VergePublishing.org

Cover artwork by Megan Phillips.

This is a work of fiction. Names, characters, places, and
incidents either are the product of the author's imagination or
are used fictitiously. Any resemblance to actual persons,
living or dead, events, or locales is entirely coincidental.

For my Father, my Mother, and those of us who find ourselves still awake at 3am

Preface

I have been writing this book for a while now. It certainly has not come together all at once. This collection has been accumulating through quite the span of ups, downs, heres and theres. But what I can promise you is that I have never written without *wanting* to write. There is no piece of work here that I have forced out, or paced over.

I recommend reading this book between the hours of 11 pm and 3:45 am as those were the hours during which most of this book was written.

And please, whenever you are lonely, need a friend, or someone to sit up with you while your thoughts race, when you can't get someone off of your mind, when you are the happiest you've ever been, whenever you are craving a cup of tea, pick up this book. These words are here for you however and whenever you need them.

So let's begin, shall we? Turn the page, I'll go start another pot of hot water…

Forward

This is heartbreak
and self-love
This is trial and error
This is everything I have felt since I was
seventeen

I have done my best to craft you
a cup of tea
a conversation
to be shared and sipped

I am offering my heart to you
so, should you need it,
you might be able to tend to your own

I believe in smiling often and crying hard. It is important to love yourself through the sun and the storms.

Best Wishes

Good morning dear
Be bold today
Be brave

The audacity to love as strongly as you
Ever have

In the face of any oncoming wind

Denny's

I could have sworn that night would be
Harmless
Nothing important has ever started or ended with
Pancakes

What was it then?
What drew the conversation to being lonely
When did I wonder how close I could be to you
Before smelling the coffee you held to warm both of
Your hands

-Thank goodness there is comic relief-
Syrup pouring faster than we'd expected
Yes, blueberries do remind me of summertime…
You've been having trouble keeping my name from your mind

Do your lips taste the same as they used to?

-Laughing again-
Because there are idiots building black holes in a lab somewhere
Because you said you are too full for toast as you take another bite
Because I'd like a little house on the moon when you'd prefer a
mansion on Mars

I know it could never be midnight forever…
But for a time I thought it might

I forgive you for letting me leave
I regret the somewhere else we had to be

Still There is Hope

Perhaps I am foolish
To search for answers in the depths of simple pleasure
I've yet to conjure anything out of the darkness
Bitter sips warn me only to be patient

Fever Dream

I imagine two bare feet
Running as fast as they can
Across a field

Just booking it into the
Woods
Until the trees start flying
Past

A sense of urgency
Not out of fear but
Necessity

Running towards a beast the
Way you'd run towards a
Sanctuary

I don't think it's being clever
Or being brave
Or being strong
Or being selfish

I think its eyes open
Following a compass North

That's how I imagine it feels to fall in love

I've been to those woods
I've stood at the edge

One of these fever dreams will
Keep hold of me in my sleep

Follow me into the morning

Dictionary

There ought to be some sort of word for what I am now
Broken and building
Solid and leaning
Open and four-walled
Wide eyed, Wall flowered
Wishing, Scarred, Scared and impatient
Clumsy, Forgiving

A hummingbird flying over the sea

Homedriven and lockless
Cautiously optimistic

Looking for lights in the dark

By now there ought to be something
For all that I am and
All I'm becoming

Image

I look in the mirror
Just for the hell of it

As in:
    Just for kicks

As in:
Sometimes it's hell to be met by a stranger

I'm never sure if that face
Is actually mine
Right away

Hair and the teeth a little out of focus

And my body
Is it mine? Is that where I am?

I've been trying to turn Hell into Hello

I take my hands
(Trembling or not)
Then carefully hold my hips and my belly

"Thank you" I spell
Plus a little heart
In the collecting steam
On the glass

Sometimes there isn't any message back

Sometimes a whisper
Sometimes there is courage and moxie
Right there in the pointillism Eden

An endless pool of patience

Lips parted in an upturned smile

Lifting all the other stories
Tied within the braid
Tangled over my shoulder

There is hope and
Forgiveness
In my outline

If canvas can stretch over sky
Paint dripping over curves and hillside
So too should the clouds form the shape of a woman

You are Beautiful

It is six o'clock in the evening
The sun was out today and is still playing lightly in the sky

The room would be hot
If it were not for the box fan spinning its wings
Briskly around in circles

We are talking about something, anything, when suddenly -
"You are beautiful"

The lights are
On
My hair has been affected by the heat and is now
Not so much a compilation of ringlets
As it is
A frayed and undefined mass defying gravity

"You are beautiful"

There is a scar on my right knee from the time
I fell running to class in
High school

A scar on my index finger from
Reaching too high
From hitting it on the corner of my
Refrigerator

"You are beautiful"

I have never had a six pack
I have never waxed my eyebrows
My lipstick has melted off in the heat

I own at least 18 different sweaters
Sometimes I get the better of my own willpower
I have an entire cupboard at home that contains
Only my collection:

Of mugs

"You are beautiful"

Now it is echoing in my ears
Through the times I've been broken, or almost, or fallen

You are beautiful beautiful beautiful you

This time last year I had only just learned your name, now it seems the only thing my mind knows how to say.

Slip

Whole and held down by my heart
Floating in space on the sidewalk
I'm not sure where I've landed:

In a world that is abstract or
In a reality hopelessly literal

The rain sings in staccato cymbals
Leaving little love notes on the frame of my glasses
I wipe the lenses on my shirtsleeve
Then continue walking down the street

We're in the thick of it

Hands tenderly grasping at monsters and shadow
Eyes buried in light

Drive on the mind
Flying in circles
Loving too hard

Leaving early

Queen Anne Cafe

Antsy feet
Lead me to the coffee shop on the hill an hour away

One I have only been to a handful of times
Times like these

There is always an intention of sitting down
Interrupted by an order to go

Always writing letters
Never to anyone I know

There are a million other things for me to do today

Tilted Frame

If it were not for the crooked picture frame
I might never have known what was wrong

If those perfectly placed corners
Hadn't been shifted
There would be nothing to notice, nothing to
Point to

No reason for me to think "yes, you see, here is proof
The words we say have a physical effect."

I would not have goosebumps from those paintings staring at me
Those walls might have felt sacred
They might have held sturdy

At least I do not fear the oncoming wind
It has already followed us inside

In the Heat of the Day

I wish very much you would try harder to understand
You cannot just stare at me for a moment
Throw your hands over your head saying you tried

I am anxious

It is easy to tell me beautiful things, believe me
They are ripe and bending your branches
I am not hungry for such fruitless labor

I am starving for purpose, for twilight

I am begging to be speechless
Inspired

Can't you hear me?
I am reaching out to you
My hands keep coming back empty

I Can't Put The Love We Shared Onto Paper

I have tried
Every time I place my pen to the paper I hear you say "Hello" for
the first time
You reach to hold my hand without any question
I start to lean on your shoulder
All of a sudden it's three in the morning and neither of us know
where the time went
Neither of us want to go home

I hear the door and your footsteps coming home from work
The gravity of your day still on your shoulders when you sleep

You keep saying that you love me
You keep asking me to change

I always write in hindsight and I always saw the both of us ahead
of me

None of it's enough
We don't know how to let each other go

How To Tell Your Boyfriend Of Three Years You Are Moving To
Alaska Without Him

Step 1: Panic.
First a little
And then…
A LOT

Make sure you are
-Alone
-In your car
-On the freeway
-In the middle of rush hour traffic

Because you, my darling, are stuck
You have already made up your mind.

DO NOT: look at the others through their window
They will not know how to help you dear, I am sorry
They will not know how to turn you around.

Step 2: Take a deep breath
Count to ten
Your mind might clear a little bit then
…
Or maybe you'll pass out
Either way you will be at peace for at least a
Little while

Step 3: (Brace for it)
Be cruel
Make him sit at the other end of the couch
Make him feel the thousand miles before it has
Even come out of your mouth
Make him
Ask you
What is wrong

Tell him it's nothing

B.S.
That he should have seen this coming
B.S
That you are only trying to fix things
B.S
Tell him that you are feeling a lot like a Caesar salad
A what?

Tossed
    ...
       a-side

Soften a bit
Tell him it was already quiet when you walked in the room
That this was already fractured

You can hope
That his hands find your hips your thighs
That his lips chase hello not goodbye
But they won't my dear,
I am sorry

He will stare at you like you are a flashing green traffic light
-Confused
-Unfamiliar
-Unsure how to proceed

It will not, my dear, be easy

Step 4: Pour some wine
Pack up your things
Take your time
Processing
That feeling,
In your stomach
You aren't afraid

There is a whole world out there for you to take on
To change
Be brave little dove

You have known all along

You should never be lonely when you are in love

What We Built on Shaky Ground

Who could have known,
                    My love

That we would lay our brick home
Too close to the ocean
Too close to the fault line

An uneven split between
Your side
                    And mine

If I thought we could land it
I'd have dived head first into our chasm

So perhaps
It is my fault

For believing darkening skies shouldn't be heavy
For casting our windows away from the storm
"Look how lovely it is on the other side of the shore"

For securing our anchor with
Rubber band rope

I thought we'd withstand it

....Almost....

White Rabbit

I feel as though I have fallen through the
Looking-glass
Or at least I had fallen through
But I have found my way out again

I feel as Lucy must have
Walking back out of the wardrobe
When her feet were once again upon the wood of the floor
Instead of the snowy wooded forest

When you carry all the change within you
But this world doesn't have anywhere for you to place it
There aren't any voices that even know to ask

How strange it is to be informed only a week has gone by
Surely by now it has been
A year

How curious to find myself missing home when
I was not sure before that I had one

From here, it could very well have been a dream
From here, it very well could still be

Didn't I do everything I was told White Rabbit?
Things, I thought, were supposed to make sense
I wouldn't leave you in the cold White Rabbit

Why do I feel without a friend?

Selfish Branches

Treacherous
          Trembling

I will follow this darkening path
I will tread deeper to the heart of this whispering hollow

Lest I be afraid

A prophecy?
A promise of light?

Only my hair in the wind
Only the warmth of my fire

I will grow my garden here
I will protect this harrowing wood

Lavender and Soft Light

At last,
The moon has let go of the mountainside

Finally
She is reflecting her luminescent music across the ocean channel
Into the blue life vein of our city
I think I can breathe again

I search the very bottom of my coffee mug

Hoping to find an extra 12oz
Somewhere behind a curtain or
Underneath a false bottom
But my cup offers me no magic this evening

Why can't I sleep?

"You don't want to"
Comes a voice
Made of lavender and soft light
"You have been pulled to my twilight
With the rest of the tide
Still,
You are hoping for answers"

Moon,
It is a strange thing
When even I cannot tell if I am honest
I have been staring at this mirror so long
I can no longer tell which side I am on

Confession: I have been closing my eyes
So tight I thought I might as well
Write this poem
In the dark

"Is it working?"

It might be

I am afraid if it is
What my heart is trying to tell me

"You," says the moon,
"Are a hopeless romantic

You are clamoring
For the magic of it

Those rose colored glasses
Are the best in the world you could find
The world looks so beautiful to you all of the time"

You know me
As you have all my life
I fear this is all my fault

Can you tell me
If that is true?

But she is low to the sky now
My eyes heavy with dawn

Fading quickly out of sight
Try as I might
I cannot support the weight of this

"Please do not go!" I am able to manage
"I will not be myself, please, I can't stand it."

"It is not up to me" She relents as she leaves
"You'll feel better with daylight
Just wait, you'll see"

With my eyes stinging red
Moon rivers drying
I crawl into bed
I pray she is right

She usually is
This time of night

A Soft Wind

I am sorry is what it whispered
I am sorry that I sometimes send you, little tender bird
Flying places you have tried to leave

I don't always mean to bluster
I trip, now and then, in the air

Do not be afraid, little tender bird
Both of us are stronger now
I will find your open wings
I will lift you

I only wish to help you fly

Maps

If every map
Became true all at once:

Written text, memory
Stone upon stone
Monsters in the sea

The land beneath rumbling from
Weathered paper
Vessels long forgotten
Letters carried by the wind

Castles hasten constitution
Mountains lifting tired heads
Forests raising fallen branches

Oceans stretch themselves
Open
Shrinking exhale
Folding onto themselves
Ten foot waves weaving
Between
Neighboured stilling water

Close your eyes
Follow the voice that
Carries you "This way"

Leave what is heavy behind

Wind's Lullaby

My Dear,

You've already found
Everything you're looking for

It's Just that now isn't
Then for you
Yet

You've all your life to sort the details

Don't waste these precious moments
Making sense

The Bar in Winter

With all of the dancing
The hot air
You'd have almost believed it was summertime

Alas, it is winter
The wind has been sweeping our spirits
Indoors

We are together
Laughing in our handmade haven
Making light of the harrowing cold
Blue whale fists

We have, already, our voices
Our music
The clinking of glasses

Gravity

Light
Pressed upon timid lips

Who told you?

The weakness of my moon spirit notions

Helpless

Luring me towards our eclipse

Merlot, My Second Glass

Sipping a burgundy merlot
I stare into my glass
I hope to be
In love

Perhaps the feeling will
Stain my stomach
The way the color
Grabs my tablecloth

My head gives way to balance
Swaying long before any music
Before my hand extends past itself
Over the table
Beyond conversation
Accepting your offer to dance

All I see is honey
My lack of it

Clover whispered softly in my ear
Summertime
The heat of both travels
slowly
    down
        my neck
Blushing a pink sky
  across
        my chest

How long will this longing persist?
How could I be as wanting as this?

Will you carry me home?
Please, will you
Quiet the noise?

I will drape myself over your shoulder
Like a wildflower clings to a hillside

My Darling,
          friend
Have I found you in this moment
Inexplicably and honestly happy

So I can say
I told you so

But I won't

Instead
There will be soft petals
Painted upon crimson lips

Perhaps I am enchanted
Maybe I am bewitched

It will be long past tomorrow morning
Before I discover which is which

Contented

The last bit of afternoon
Filters past open spaces
Wherever the living room curtains
Will allow it

The sun a ripened peach
Now too heavy for the sky's
Branches

This is when
You say you see the shapes of me even
With your eyes closed

I let your voice hum around
The air awhile
Blending sweet nothings with
Slices of honeycrisp apple

There isn't any hurry here

My Alaskan Heart

Wild like this place
That undertow
That fierce craving for
Both anchor and freedom
That evergreen
Full forward
Full stop

<u>February 1, 2017</u>

What a fitting first evening in February
Pastel
Cotton candy

Both reflect their youthful circles
Across my eyes

Thank God I am swimming in light

The moon is here,
As is Neverland's waters

Try as I might to blend into this landscape
It is far too fragile for me

Oh my stars
I am living in a dream

Quietly

I think about you quietly
Like the slow and steady ambience of a clock
Tick-tocking down to when
I might see you again

Up until now
The tea cup and its contents have remained
Too-hot-to-drink for us

Stubborn as we are
We have sipped defiantly from it anyway

While that elixir radiates upon our restless lips
We suffer from our burning tongues

Are we distracting ourselves

With other conversation, other company
While we wait

Is that why I feel so impatient?

It is so easy to hold onto a cup of tea though, isn't it
The comfort of warm hands
Delays the promise of an empty cup

While I know we cannot last forever
I would rather sip slowly
Than risk us growing cold

Vague Incentive Vagabond

Sweet Nectar
Tugging at my sleeve
Eyelids fighting off the floating shapes
Indigo
Diving deep
Surrounding myself with drift and sensation
Giving in
Carried by the upper river
Blurring lines of heart and mind

Bookstore Bowtie

Darling
the way it rolled off of your tongue like diamonds

Rouge
the way my cheeks filled with heat behind the books I hid in

Midnight
the way we didn't need it, dancing in living rooms

Secrets
the way we fell towards each other in a twilight of
lowered voices

Beautiful
the way I remember you in colors and in autumns

Heartbreak
the way we didn't mean to, the way we wish we could be different

Messes
the way we left things, the both of us

Selfish
the way I asked you to kiss me just one more time
the way you looked into my eyes
the way you rested your hands softly on either sides of my
cheekbones

I'd never been held in a moment that way

Cigarette smoke
Coffee gone cold

I don't allow myself to think of you
More than in pieces
I have been doing my best to stitch you back
Into the pages

You see, even now
You are still my favorite story

I wonder often if you miss me

I think you are the reason I run towards a setting sun

Kids like us, we don't know when to stop. Thank goodness for this, we never give up.

To Be Us

Bright Eyes
Bloodshot at the bus stop
French fries, empty cans
Superman on our lunchbox

Late nights
Dark disguise for the streetwise
Starlight
Morse code lullabies
We swear we're the only ones who hear it

We are young
We are young
We are young

Welcome to the planet parade
A drunken mishap
The grand charade

We will live long with the moon
So long as the sun stays low
So long as today stays far away from tomorrow

Today we are young
We are young
We are young

The future
Ain't as bad as it seems
I can toast to that
There isn't time to think

Of the money
Of the rent
Of the time we have spent
Where we are going
Or what lies ahead

They say we are free
As we are chained to a desk
Bordered
With a windowless fence

So let us be
Let us stay golden and naive
While we can

While we are young
We are young
We are young

Stumbling into Strong Arms

The second you picked me
When you tilted your head
Ever so slightly to the right

It's as clear as when it happened
I fill my cup half full with that siren song whenever it is empty

Your hands on my waist
Fingers pulling my edges towards you
Like you're the North star
Like we're eighteen

Your lips
As close as they can at the edge of together

When you asked me to stay
I watched the words take shape for an instant
Evanescent

The wanting never goes away

Blushing and Beaming

I wonder
In this moment
If I could have been
Anywhere else in the world
And been half as happy

I'm not sure I have known such a feeling before this

Lifted

Tied to my hand is a star shaped balloon
Clockwise, around the circumference of my wrist

The balloon reaches
Aiming for the sky

I had hoped this would be enough to lift me
But I am only keeping it closer to the ground

Flights not Feelings

If you are telling me
That all of us know where we are going
I can assure you now you are wrong

There is no promise that any of our steps will even land on the
floor in front of us

In the air
At least we do not need to pretend
We will place our bags above or below us
We will hope we did not forget our
Pens or our chargers

We will wonder about the strangers sitting next to us
Not enough to speak

The only thing firm on our minds:

At least there is proof we are moving, even while we are sitting
still

Lincoln Station

I find myself drawn to the station
The ghosts of them
The whistle blowing loudly
The clicking of steel horses upon an iron earth

I find myself running
Urgency of the white rabbit
A side effect of my romantic notions

I stand at the platform
Waiting
A good half an hour before I accept the tracks no longer function

I'm still shaking off that phantom dream

Indigo Bridge Bookstore

I was out wandering again, as I often do
Neither searching for place
Nor searching for purpose

Rather, settling in to my restless tendency

I had no particular reason to look up when I did, but these little
windows called me over

I'd found a little haven built into the brick
I'd found others with spines bound in paper & prose

I tended and mended my spirit before setting out again
Floating on a cloud out the door

<u>1am</u>

I keep my eyes open
In case I see something allowing my mind to
Breathe easy

I keep them closed
Against that impractical idea
Fascinating fantasy

Truth is I'm not sure what I am looking for
Or if it even exists

But my shadow is searching

Searching
Searching
Searching

Robert Frost Keeps His Secrets (From Me At Least)

Two paths diverged in a yellow wood
And I?

I've been standing here for a week now

A month now

I've made a nest here
I'm not allowed to build a home here
So I don't
But I try

I sing lullabies and war songs
I read a lot
I worry with clenching fists
I tidy the leaves

It rains like a mother who dotes on their child
The sun stokes my courage like a darkening fire

The wind is soft
But pushing all the time

I fall in love
I fall over
I tether sticks together for shelter

They hold me as a lover
Or a friend
Never both

Never meant to be more than a visit
So I don't give those woods a name anymore

They call me weary traveler
They call me starry bluebird
They call me from branches at three in the morning:

Lovely girl
Miss Hollywood
Poor thing
Pretty thing

I scratch the titles into the walls and the door frame

I leave my maps in pieces under the floorboards
Paint upon the windows

In case anyone else can make sense of them

Drop-and-Shatter

I wanted to stop caring for you
You know?

I thought I just would when the time came
Drop-and-shatter of sorts

Now I just hold the pieces to the light
Turning the memories into pretty colors

I sit in this missing-of-you
Wanting, Withholding
A promise not to look too closely

I tilt my head to the left just-so
I bite my lip
I pull the end of my curls straight then watch them bounce towards
me again

In how many ways can I be pulled closer and away I wonder

I save chocolate and wine for the worst of it
I hold onto bitter coffee like it's both the answer and the question

Would you like to meet for a minute
Would you like to sit on other ends of the earth and pretend that
we're strangers
Would you like to come over
Would you like to be alone
With me

I might leave my lipstick print on an empty glass
Then your tie
Then your neck
Then…

I'd like to never think of you again
I'd like to fall into anybody else
I'm trying to

Tell me:

Have you forgotten what it was to lie to each other?

Our kind of reverie doesn't come around all the time

The music's been keeping me up at night
Driving me wild into the old pine
Into strong arms

Tracing my silhouette with a whisper
Holding just the distance in our hands

Safe harbor like a candle in soft wind
I bend my body 'round the flame
Protecting pretty light keeps my mind off
How long the nights are

Voices and Ivy

Those vines made it up
The walls before
The wolves ever could

I'd have clambered over too had I been able

Had I heard them coming

There's a kind of peace once you accept being lost in the maze

Truth is I feel dull in the daylight

It is best to grow into the madness

Howl along with the rest of them

If I Were the Roses I'd Tell You

Do not hold in your bloom for fear of an autumn

Follow the heat

You've eyes even when they aren't open

Your heart will guide you towards the sun

The Problem Is:

I'm not good with broken hearts
I've not been taught how to tend to the
Mending

Just the hurt
Just the stamps from the roses
Just the mourning of petals on the ground

<u>Clover</u>

Reach little clover

Wander wherever you wish

Do not wait for another or beg them to stay

Love never had much to do with counting leaves anyway

The Giant

I'd not gone anywhere in particular
I'd just seen the clock had a little room
I took advantage of all the new
Free of any comfort from habit
I found the brick and I followed it

…

The street fell away
Little sounds from the traffic and the townsfolk
Feathered weather shade
Passing over the sun
Just enough so I knew what I'd lost and what I gained again

…

That's when I came upon the giant
That's when I fell apart a little, then back together
That's when I didn't know where my words went or
What to do with my arms

…

I offered "Hello," and a question
He answered:
"It's just the space in between
That's what's hitting so loudly
It's alright to be strange, the world's enough space for the color
It's alright, wayfaring sparrow, the world's enough space for a
home
These are the tools that fix your heart."

<u>Sidewalk Pigeon</u>

Sometimes I'm caught in the rain like this
A little lost
A little smaller than the rest of the world

I don't know if it means
Belonging lies in the hands of my
Perception

Or

If I am just looking for a face
In the grey

Hot Chocolate

Subtle notes of home
Wrapped in porcelain
I dive into the white noise
The hearthside
Leaving the rain and the wind a foreigner
Beyond the glass

I am warmed within and
Amber incandescence
Chocolate bloom
Savored bitter-sweet

The mulled moment nestled
Within the haze of an early
Afternoon

Frost

3am
The witching hour
Winter chill is, at last, allowed to
Draw herself from the shivering air
Lifting fractals & fragment

.

Tenderly
Fragile arms and elbows embrace
Rooftops, pine trees, fences, meadows

.

Soft
Longing kisses left on windows
Painting all the world in frozen blossom
(She has heard so much of spring)

.

Delicate frame
Taking care not to weigh down what's beneath her

All the Lies that Lead us Here

The bar is empty
Except for your glass of
Whisky on the table and
My glass of wine half-full

I'd have finished it but

You fell in love with me

I pull the glass from my lips

You didn't mean to

I place the glass on the table

You're glad that you did
You wish that you hadn't

In the end none of it matters

I tug at my sleeve
I bite at my lip
I pull at my hair

It's just a dull ache that I carry around

Casablanca

I dance with the very thought of you
Memories tucked within an envelope of time and care

Dawning my best dress
Champagne in a long stem
Cheers darling
There's a war out the window

Sober or not
He has so much trouble making sense of me

We sit on either side of the table
We stand on other sides of the city
We sleep on other sides of the coastline
None of it helps

Here's lookin' at you kid

<u>There is a Man at the Airport</u>

Who looks exactly like you

The posture
The stature
The angle of the chin
The way that he acts like a
Stranger

In fact
From this far away
With my glasses still missing
I've convinced myself that
You found me

We're just deciding not to
Speak here

For the convenience of it
For the thrill
For fear and for bravery
For nothing at all

Why not be
Blurry and silent at the airport
Why not scale the wanting
The probability and
Impossibility to the confines of
20ft

Either way
I catch the next flight out

And

You let me

Don't mind me, I'm just hurling myself into vulnerable situations and screaming into the void

Metro Thoughts

A gust
   Stumbles
Tongue-tied and tripping through the
Platform

Before the train hits the station
At 10:42pm
Just when I think that
I've missed it

Rails clack like the steam from my kettle

A mouse scurries

Hair on my shoulder falls loose from
Its half-hearted braid

I make space on the crowded car

Leaning heavily against a corner of the
Tired wall
Using only the left of my shoulder blade

I try not to think of who might be
Thinking less of me

We gather in silence
A collective decision to exist invisibly

Traveling Still

Weary traveler
In the hum of such high ground
Within the bridges and rivers
You've your own restless intentions

Worry
Ache
Rest

Project yourself over the glass
Shoulder and hands in the train car

Flowers

The flowers on the windowsill
Still know better than I

When the sun decides it cannot stay
They're not afraid to say goodbye

She is:

Treading lightly

Tracing paths made from
Pastel
    Petals
        And paper

Could you blame her?

For embracing such
Reckless abandon
Dancing with cause and
Distraction

She is dizzy
She is full of breath

Uncovering mirage and mâché

Spring Rain

I would answer all her
Questions if I could
Spring rain doesn't really
Need them though
Answers, I mean

There's one million things to
Care about
Besides

She'll laugh and toss her hair back
Weaving worries into
Ribboned lace

I tip-toe so as not to
Startle any stories off

Though I confess
I could never listen long enough

Violet Morning

Purple haze covered every inch of the outstretching landscape
Soft shaded violet kissed the hilltops
Blanketing the valleys with
A heavenly mist

It was easy, on this occasion, to believe
No one was awake yet
That the earth might be in love
~ It was spring after all ~

I blushed as much as the morning
It seems we are alike in our shyness
How I wished to be free and unbound by
My limited tongue

Dawn,
I am awestruck
I am breathless
I know now why cherries blossom
With soft petals and rouge

La Vie en rose my darling
I will pray to see you soon

A Love like Ours

Never before
Had "Hello" sounded more to me like
Walking in from a cold winter snow
To the warm amber glow of a bookstore
You knew how to hold me that way

I am handed "Lovely Girl" and
"Sweetheart" in a long stemmed glass of
Burgundy wine
I prefer staying tipsy to sober
Can you feel the both of us spilling over

Kiss me darling
Again
And again
And again

We'd been caught in our own kind of gravity
I will stay lost for as long as you'll have me

The Fairweather

They say a sailor hears a
Siren's call
Then follows her into the ocean

I believe them

Those waters at the
Shoreline know more than
They're telling
They keep me near the coast

That voice caught hold of my
Name somehow
It catches and crashes as
Dissonant waves against my teeth

I'm not sure where my mind is anymore
Just chasing that melody of blue

I'll spend my whole life
Wondering where that song is coming from

<u>I know</u>

Love isn't supposed to
Look the same every time

Waiting for lightning to strike the same place twice just
Leaves me lonely

Message in a Bottle

I miss
    You
More than I ought to
More than this timid heart should allow

Keep me afloat
Wind waters

Tangle me tighter in the spell of your tidepool
I don't think I'd care if I ever saw land again

Wandering sailor
I could be your home

Since You Left

"I love you"
Recently
Looks a lot like:

Crossed out letters in my notebook

.

Hurling a message-in-a-bottle
To the ocean

.

Holding my breath

.

Staying awake

.

Anything other than saying it really

Spilling Over

I wish I could breathe in color
So I could better explain my mind

I wish I could shape shift or
Paint myself onto
Canvas

I no longer feel myself in solid form
I no longer know how to sit still

My pens have been missing the paper
My words have been missing their mark

Do you think the woods would take me back?

If the sunlight would filter through my weathered skin
As it does through the branches

Would I understand then
Which pieces of myself are whole
And which pieces I have only imagined?

Waking Up to Him

I have this compilation of
Half-awake memories

I reach for him and
He's there
And
Heaven is on Earth

Then I am asleep again
I feel him kiss my forehead

It is all so hazy and warm and
Wonderful

I am dreaming,
  even in the daylight.

Museum

Now and again
I catch myself
Not in any particular fashion
Not in any particular light

Simply
Holding the pieces
Looking for likeness
Pulling at threads

If I ever wake up
I'll place timid bare toes onto iced hardwood floor
To be sure

If the shock of the cold doesn't shake me

Say only this:

"Good morning my love
We are out of the woods
You're of body and mind, not of canvas
There's not any need to wait anymore"

Paper Wings

I cried as the little moth
Went from the cold to the
Fire
Like it was an answer
Or a gift

I cried

Because I couldn't fault the
Fire
For being what it was

Then

Another pair of wings

Pale
Delicate
Deliberate

"Why,"
I cry out
"Why does the flame draw you so fiercely?"

Sometimes they pause
Sometimes they rest on my shoulder
Sometimes they don't pay me any mind

The answer is always the same

"Why shouldn't I wish to be warm?"

Rationalize

I could be in love with the evening
It might explain why I grow anxious towards
The end of day
Why I am drawn towards my window

I will never know why my hands grip tighter
On the steering wheel
When all that is behind me is
A beautiful life

Vagabond

It is not your fault my dear
Distance calls to you with such urgent alarm bells
Let your hands touch softly your keys and
Contemplation

Let your eyes fix a little harder on the skyline
Unravel all the tension from the string
You have spun for yourself

You do not owe your past a trail of breadcrumbs

Feel the weight of all that is behind you

Allow for that force to carry you forward

Simple Truths

Simple truths tied up in knots
On crumpled paper

Gin and tonic
Sipped to ice and
Heavy glass

Quiet winds from
Farther north warn me of
Midnight

But I leave that tender voice
To bitter light
Cobbled streets and
Marbled towers promise an answer

So I ask why hearts like mine
Are built of glass

They tell me
Birds sing pretty songs
But fire always leaves them restless

It's left my head a mess
My mind a compass rose

I cling to hope
And songs of old
To keep me warm

Wandering Heart

Perhaps
The relief of such motion
Came to her not in surprise
But rather softly

As warm tea on the porch in the summer
As a cat at the foot of the bed
As rain on the top of the tin roof

Imminence

Outstretch your hand
It's always a little farther than you'd expect
How illusive solid rock can be

.

Build your walls again
Find peace in solitude
Wrap ivy and wildflower 'round your eyes
To keep the light in

.

"I love you"
Climbing 'round your ankles
Grasping onto your ledges
That kind of bear will roar over your echoes
That kind of arrow will find you

Full Circle

Full circle
Looks a lot like autumn leaves
And iced coffee
Even though it's cold outside
Peeking out from a long scarf
Wishing I'd remembered the gloves my
Grandmother bought me
Digging cold hands deep into my pockets

Wishing I remembered my very first home
Phone number
I wonder if that old house would like to know
I'm in the neighborhood

If I called
Do you suppose a little me would answer
Would she say hello in a way that sounds like
Wild strawberries

Would she approve of what I've done with our youth

Self-Care

Sometimes self-care is being the first customer
At Donna's Diner

I'll never tell anyone why I tried to sleep
In my car, or the million reasons why
Sleep never came

But you can imagine the relief of those warm lights
The maple walls
Green booth trim
A sign reading:
"Seat yourself"
I am not a bother here

No one else has arrived yet
But Cher is asking urgently if I believe
In life after love through the old speakers

I hate that the answer is
Yes

Even now

Still, I muffle a laugh in my hand
Until the waitress wanders over

She does not ask me how I am doing
She does not ask why I had to use the
Decor mirror on the wall to wipe off last night's
Makeup

She offers instead a single word
The one I've been dreaming of since the
Midnight before

"Coffee?"

"Yes please."

I don't even notice the menu
On the table
Until she has left me with
My hands clasping
To the plain white mug radiating
Life back into my
Body

6 AM

Dark roast at the start of the daylight
As quiet honey hues lift gently over the break of the mountain
So too does my spirit stretch into my skin

I will hold close my breath and my worry
Until it can lift from my lips as the
Steam from my cup

The mysterious cloak of the morning
The milk dancing in circles in darkness
My cheeks getting warmer and rosy
The heart on the roof of my mouth

I will sit in this moment of stillness
I will savor bitter sips on my tongue

In truth
It's the kind of love
I can't live without

The Nature of Ivy

In my garden it is wicked
Roots left too long
Embedding over and under in satisfied knots
Vines lashing from soil to
My eyes
Surroundings slip to
Memory before I even blink

Before I lead myself to water

I get it:

-Sometimes letting go can kill you
-Sometimes nothing is enough

I try to voice my worry as an antidote
But there is no language of this for the ivy
I have nothing else to give

Wild Voice of the Darkest Wood

Silly animal
Haven't you been lost long enough
Haven't you grown tired

That river is in you now I can see it
You're hooked on the river now
You need it

The air though
Has it cleared for you
Can you breathe it

Do you dare to
Would you believe it

Silly a n i m a l
You are hiding
Abiding to
Laws you think you can run from

That sun will blind even you
If you stare
         Too
            Long

Didn't I tell you
You'd find yourself lost here?

You are lost
Aren't you dear

The water is cold on your hungry hands
The wolves are at your heels love
They wish to turn you into sand

Silly animal
You still don't understand

You never stood a chance

She Ties a Tie

Staring at the mirror she analyzes the bareness of her neck
The soft skin partially hidden by her
Upturned collar

In her hand she holds a long piece of fabric
Its uneven distribution
Unfamiliar to her fingers

She places the cloth around her neck
Lifting her hair out and over the
Foreign fabric

Steps muttered under her breath as she
Ties the knot and pulls it towards her throat
Tying, then untying, retrying until the knot looks

Respectable
Ordinary
Uniform

Is this what it takes to be listened to?

Feeling every sentence she says
She realizes how easy it would be for someone
To grab hold of the string and
Pull
Choking her on her own words

"It would still be my fault" she marvels
"It would still, somehow, be my fault."

Me Too

"It must be weird to be a woman"
The sentence cascades from my significant other
On the car ride home from dinner

"Knowing every guy could probably hurt you... probably."

For a minute I cannot speak
It is just quiet

"It would be like walking around a bear all the time and constantly
hoping they
Aren't dangerous"

I stare out of my window
Observing the dusk turning swiftly into night
Trying to deny that I feel
So much safer with him there

But I do

Yes
It can be like that

Then something inside of me snaps
I think it started to crack at seventeen
With my hand on the doorknob
When my mother told me:
"You look beautiful! Be careful"

When I was first taught that boys were better at math
That my weight matters more than my ability
That the probability
Of earning less than any man
In any occupation
Is a reality of
79 cents to every dollar

I tell him about this past week

About the man who shouted crude things
From the bus stop
About what he would like to do to my body
I tell him about walking alone down Eagan Drive
About the man who
Pulled his red truck to the side
Rolled his window down and told me to get in
So he could drive me the rest of the way into town
How after telling him no
He circled the block until our eyes locked again
Until he found me
Windows still down
Eyes still hungry

I tell him

City bears are not afraid of the daylight
They will reach out and grab my waist
At the coffee shop

And worse
They can do so much worse
But that's a nightmare I'm not ready to talk about yet

"What did you do when this happened?"
My wide-eyed love asks me
Keeping his hands held tight
On the steering wheel

I smile
Or I stare straight ahead
I tell them I am sorry
That is how I have been taught to survive

It is quiet again
But this time
He did not tell me that I should be more careful

There is No Title

Someone grabbed me
On Saturday
I wasn't alone
I was looking away
I was wearing a skirt
So they had the freedom I guess
And it was only a second, you know?
It was only their hand there and then gone
It was only my eyes searching for answers then finding their own -
and a wink
Oh my god do you know what that felt like?
That I must relive that this happened with the burden of an
asterisk
That I could only process a million things at once:
1. No
2. And it's a stranger
3. And they are looking at me
4. And they're smiling
5. And they know what they've done
6.
Seconds,
it was only six seconds between this and the door, and *I did*
I said stop
I said wait.
And I did
I ran to authority-I told him "That man,
the one who is standing outside now
who is smoking a cigarette
he just
grabbed me,
I don't want to say where,
I don't know who he is"

To be met with
"I'm sorry,
you should have done something before he made it outside,
I can't do anything now."
It was only myself thinking no,
It was only myself saying no,

It was only myself saying **fuck you**,
going outside to face him
So I stood there and I found his eyes again they were startled this
time, they were nervous this time
Do you believe me
When I say there were 5 that I challenged, that there were 5 that
stood - lighting his cigarette
There were 5 that just stared and said nothing
Do you believe me when I say I was alone on the sidewalk

"Hey!"
- "I'm sorry"
"You don't get to do that!"
- "I'm sorry"
**"No, you don't get to touch other people without their
permission"**
The cigarette sits alight in his mouth
- "I'm sorry"
"Don't be sorry just—"
- "I'm sorry"
"Don't ever do that again."

I sink my heels into the dirt of the unfinished pavement
I have not slayed a dragon
I have not slowed a beast
I have howled my aggression into violent wind
I will never know where it lands

The Difference

Things are different in the dark
It does not matter how long something has stood in either sunlights
or midnights,
Nothing is ever the same in one as it is in the other

I would like to think I can be strong in both
That I am not blinded by either

But moments like these tell me days have been sunny
And I have been going to bed on time

While it is a simpler task to distinguish
Dark from the light

I am having a harder time
Distinguishing
Perseverance from Pride

An Ode

I add an inch to my heels for every boy who's ever told me
"I wish you weren't taller than I am"

I've begun soaking rain through my skin

"But you are already so tall" - as they elevate the angle of their chin

"But you are already so tall" - as they climb the abyss of my branches

"But you are already so tall" - as they yell from the tops of the mountains

"But you are already so tall" - as they send their signals into space

I will grow green in spite of your cliffsides

I will grow green in spite of your deserts

My legs are only getting longer

My roots ever deeper in the earth

I've not become nor undone
  Rather, there is a way things are and a way they are perceived

  In either case I feel more than I can carry

Beaming Effluence

Dearest Moon,

It seems I'm in your light again

Dissolve me quicksilver
Dripping wolves in the ocean

A trail of whispers

Howling
Hungry
Luminescent

Castles in the Air

Bear with me
I am still only half-awake

I have not yet found the boundaries

My hands gripping the fraying edges of the map
What is real
What I have only imagined

Evenings in Earnest

Share with me the reddest sun you've ever seen
The storms you bring
The creases in your sheets

But please
Nothing of the scars you've gotten

Let your skin be your skin again

I will hold you close all the same

Written During the Head and the Heart Concert on the Roof of
Pike Place Market

We all lean out the window
As the sun sets
Music fills the alley
As our lungs and our fists
Shake in the air
Nothing is for sale today

They'll feel us after this
Even after we've made our way
Home
Gathered together
Howling and singing
Sending our hearts to the
City
Feet on the brick at the
Market

I Couldn't Sleep so I Wrote this Instead

There was a quiet knock on the door
One that might have been the wind
Or a distant tap of thunder

I opened the framework
Out of habit
And hope
Unassuming

Instead appeared
Every letter I had almost written
Right there on the front porch

All the ink still inside my pen
The tideline
And moonlight

It was you

We said hello like we'd been lovers
We kept each other warm for a while
Company like muted violins
Coloring the space with dahlias and honey

"So you've withstood the time and the distance"
"So you're just as I remember, and the pull is still the same"

Neither was sure who could tend to this matter completely
Or put it to rest

If it was question
Accusation
Or compliment

No way to fold it neatly

So we placed the thought
Between us on the table until it
Found some legs of its own

We laughed to distract from
Not knowing what to do with our hands
So we could act like we
Weren't strangers still
So we could act like we
Loved each other a little less

I still can't place the beginning
I'd believe we just appeared from the air
As we have been
As we are still
As we will be?

That's when the town square wavered
Brushing the red brick with dawn
The bells were distant, but they were enough

I was left with soft piano and the rain on the rooftop
Coffee cold in ceramic
Steady footing in a dream

Bear

It's in our heads
The both of us

When the raven sings
When we are wrapped in the quiet of the night

I have felt the warmth of your breath
On the back of my neck

I have placed my hands in fallen snow

Isn't it lovely
Falling so softly
Treading slowly in the cold

It's the bear of you

The bear of you
The bear of you

Second Nature

There was a way
That his sleepy voice would carry
Over the ocean of the bedsheets

How that solid tender hand of his would
Reach blindly through the dark

To find myself
And my body
And find us every time

A rise and fall to his chest that would lull us both to sleep

Please do not speak to me of love

Do not remind me of the roses or the long drives
We'll wind up running 'round in circles again

I fear the drift
The tendency
The butterflies

I fear defining something that was never mine

Shelter

I embrace the moment for a little while longer

Like a window holds onto raindrops
Once the clouds fade away

I do not make a promise
I do not hold my breath

I pay attention to everything at once
I protect whatever stays

Breakfast

I figured it out

The glass is half full
Officially
Absolutely
Endless

As the waiter fills it back to the brim
Anytime I reveal exactly half of the ceramic wall

I have been over caffeinated for an hour
But I don't want to ruin a good thing

I am reminded
The best place to watch the sunrise is
From a booth at the table next to the window
Of the neighborhood diner

Silverware chimes harmonize with running
Water in the kitchen
And the register printing receipts near the front door

Sometimes breakfast is church

Safeguard

"These things take so much time and care"

I am reminded
I repeat it
Chewing on the words like gum

Uncertain
If I am better off

For every time I have tried again

But I believe in showing up

I know love within persistence

Flood follows footsteps

Timid or not

Harbor

I have felt both love and ice from the ocean
As it surrounds me ankle and knee
As I am pulled over and under in its wake

Follow me home
Follow me home

I have fallen in love with your spirit

In the Garden

They did not seem to mind I too was not a flower

There was a love we shared

An understanding of the way things are

Little Things

We exchange glances
Only glances

Your hand on my waist for
Only a second

But it's all at a standstill
Isn't it
The tension building into
Icebreak

It's all those little things
Adding up to
Gravity
Spring

An evocation in fervor
In appetite
In longing

We can quiet the noise
But we can't quite shake it off

All those little spells you are casting

Clouds in the Spruce Trees

There are days
I too wish to fade into the forest
Wrap myself like liquid
Around such sturdy branches

Oh my, gentle creature
    Settle my heart
        Steady my breathing

Hush the wind with your whispering song

<u>Awake</u>

I like being
Here

I like being held in the conversations of others
The chatter a bar holds

A cup setting down on the
Counter
Laughter
Talking-too-loud
Eyes across the room
Leaning closer
The cue on the 8 ball

Have you ever been warmed
Just from stepping inside a place?

I toy with the stem of a
Cherry

I let everyone go
All of them

Not to be stronger
Not to be weak
Just to see what it's like
Without a raincoat
Without any almost

I'm not disappointed
Or enamoured

I'm just sat on the edge of a barstool

Content

In one piece

Change in the Air

It wasn't the stroke of twelve
Nor the start of the witching hour

(As it so often had been)

It was eight thirty in the morning

That's when the sun caught
Its light in the fields
Spinning desert grass into
Gold

Breathing rosy cheeks into
The brick of the Sacramento Station

Shadows and rivers
Stretching like black cats
In the heart of October

As though the spell that
Drew from her lips could
Only be spoken

With the pull of the iron
Beneath her

Thundering into the dawn

River Story

Daybreak
Timid and blushing
Asks the Seine if she is
Awake yet

The Seine,
Unfolding sleepy eyes
Gives in to the light and the songbirds
Admitting
"Yes, I am awake"

So the dawn tells river stories
Doing what she can to spill the
East into the still frame

She paints what she can on the water

That river loves stories
Let me tell you
She reflects very carefully
Two elders who sit
Holding hands by the stream
As they have for fifty years

The two carry on this way
The way you do after a thousand years of falling in love

Lavender current
Peony sky
A quiet enchantment
A spring rain

Cumulus notions
Leading lost lovers
To shelter

One Mile Up

There's magic here
I'm sure of it

The very idea of magic ought to be enough proof of itself

You cannot convince me
My veins were not fashioned after rivers
Or that my thoughts
Do not construct themselves
Into a stop motion paint brush
Sending pointillism watercolor dashing freely through
Open plains

Perhaps I cannot point to a broom
To make it sweep on its own accord

But I have felt the most amazing sense of completeness

For that

There is nothing you could pay me

You deserve to feel whole. To feel that you are yourself, always. I fear though, this will not be interpreted in the way I intended. Feeling whole does not necessarily mean feeling happy, or satisfied, or 'ok'. It means that regardless of where you are in your life, you are able to accept all that you are as a living, breathing, thoughtful spirit. We are creatures of change. **Just because you are not the same now as you were in the past does not mean that at any point you have stopped being yourself.**

In solitude or in company, find this completeness however you can.

"Hello?"

A timid question
Spoken only into silence and
Dark spaces
Always with the risk of
Giving oneself away

Fully transcribed,
Neatly tucked within its
Vulnerable implication:

"I am here, are you?"
"Am I alone?"

See Subcategories:
   -I am uneasy
      &
   -I have been lonely

<u>"Hello!"</u>

A state of affairs
A declaration
A welcomed meeting

"I am here, you are here
Despite how wide the world is"

This exchange
However bold
However subtle
Holds prophecy

This statement ties red
String around each of our
Ankles

Complimentary accents:
-Again
    &
-At last

<u>There I stood</u>

With such reckless simplicity
With such vibrant color
Perhaps there can be love such as this

Plesiosaurus

Fabled ghost
I'll neither blink nor turn the lights out
I know that legendary stronghold
That pull for open water
That bite of time and patience
You've instilled inside these
Old bones

I Gave in to the Wild Wolf

He stood, too patient
Outside my door

Silent and steady

As I paced impatient circles
Into the wood of the floor

I know I'm the fool
I know

Big teeth
Carve vision and matter
        Forest and fire

Until the hinged division
Didn't matter
Anymore

I'd let myself out
He'd let himself in
Semantics

"How did you find me?
How could you love me?
When did you first learn my name?"

"Darling flood follows
Gravity
You've been talking in your sleep
We have always been one and the same."

...

I let the rain fall cold
Through my skin a moment
I let breath steady shaking hands

Calm the dissonance of mind and body

Allowing self-syncopation to settle in

I let that creature walk at my side through the mist
Gathering in pools at our
Ankles

The-middle-of-the-night
Ringing through my chest as
A thousand doves in the sky
As ripples in a tide pool
As a name

We walk
  We howl
    We run

Deeper to shadow and pine

Pursuing the heart of the forest

Garden Gate

The dawn broke above
The roses first
The dew drops they lifted with their
Delicate petals, thorns

Then the Ivy
Vibrant green and golden
Bold persistent climbing
When the sun, at last,
Above was fully shining

I found myself full of blossoms strong and rooted

I've been growing ever since

Then it Happened all at Once

I just felt so goddamn young
And it was heaven
I was human
I was listening to music in the kitchen
I was lace
I was red velvet cake
Golden rosé satin
Bottle of champagne

I didn't need anything else

Serendipity

I pick up a nectarine at the
Farmers market
The skin like a bruise
Or a sunset
Sits in my hand so honestly
I begin to separate the parts of myself
That are plastic

The first bite

I wait a little longer before it happens
Because I'm blushing
And I want to pay attention
And I've got to let my guard down

Until anticipation
Like a canary in a clock tower
Rings the bell

"Before! Before! Everything else was before!"

It's not that I couldn't wait any longer then
Rather, anything else didn't make sense anymore

-I'm laughing
-The flavor is spilling over
-It is particularly warm for an autumn's eve
-A piano is being played upon the sidewalk

But even the first bite
Is never as good as the second
Because it's someone saying they fell in love with you twice
And they meant it

Drove from Seattle to LA in 20 Hours

I decided I should drive home instead of flying
I didn't want my feet so far from the earth anymore

There's a whole lot of my spirit on the highway, a lot of questions
I shouted out the window in case the world was listening, in case it
had an answer

I am, of course, even further in awe of our planet
Of its patience and intricacies
That soft humming silver Southern Oregon,
Like a spell and a lullaby from lips barely parted
Sweet nothings and secrets resting in the hills

Mount Shasta coy and cumulative,
Like all those love notes I never sent came alive
Like they all wrote back to me with the river and I just never
thought to look before

Then the desert
The sky
Open and honest
Bold space accepting all that weight I carried with me
All that space for letting go

All I know is that I did it
I didn't stop and I didn't sleep
I hit the city running and I thank god there is all this room to run

Acknowledgements

I would like to extend my deepest thanks to everyone who helped guide this book into the world long before I even knew that I would write it.

Thank you to my parents for more than I can write. What I can write now is this: It was because of them that one of the first things I knew about myself was that I loved to read.

Thank you to my teachers:

Ms. Kypreos, when we left on the last day before summer, you wrote each student notes of encouragement. In mine you wrote "Send me a copy of your first book." As I went through any period of doubt with this manuscript I remembered the letter and thought "No, this has to come together, I've got to send her a copy."

Mr. Trafford,
Thank you for teaching your class how to engage with a story, how to understand the layers within a text. Thank you for showing us the poem about the deer even though I cried the whole time, I had not known a poem could make me feel anything before then. Thank you for truly rooting for your students and creating a class I consistently looked forward to.

Mr. Curtis,
Thank you for teaching me everything was worthy of analysis. Newspaper articles, photographs, short stories. I have since found poetry from each of these sources and now I find inspiration everywhere. Thank you for being a W.S.M.F (W.S. Merwin Fan) I will be one forever. Two years after your class I ate a plum from a small market in Dublin and that was the first time a poem has leapt from a page into my life.

Professor Leising,
Thank you for having each of your students keep poetry journals. I kept mine going after your class, that's all this really was in the beginning. Some of those poems are in here.

Thank you to Christy NaMee Erickson, DeeJay Derago, Mike Christienson, Bill Merk, Erika Bergren, Naaweéiyaa Tagaban, and Jasz Garrett, and Ms. G. Thank you for Woosh Kinaadeiyi. Thank you for your friendship and your inspiration, you were there through every page and continue to be.

Thank you to Elizabeth Rumfelt for helping me edit and make sense of the hundred pages I had printed and strewn across my living room floor. Thank you also for your continued friendship and excitement for my work.

To Juneau, Alaska, Gunanchéech. I will be forever in awe of your beauty and in debt to the Tlingit people who have shared their beautiful land with me.

To anyone who may have picked up this book and wondered if these poems were about them: they are. Thank you for the time we shared. Please know that if I had known "Goodbye" really meant "Goodbye" I might have said anything else.

To Paul and Raven, thank you for believing in both myself and this manuscript. I love being a part of this new Verge Publishing family and I cannot wait to see what the next chapter holds for all of us.

About the Author

Audrey Kohler is a poet and performer with deep roots in the Pacific Northwest and Southeast Alaska. Her work has been featured in The Juneau Empire, "The Fear Journal" compiled by Kaitlin Ruby, and has appeared as a recurring guest on KTOO'S "Telling Tales with Ms.G." She has performed with Unexpected Productions, L.A Connection, and the Juneau Lyric Opera. She studied creative writing at the University of Alaska Southeast and served on the Board of Directors of Woosh Kinaadeiyí in Juneau, Alaska before moving to Los Angeles. This is her first book.

Made in the USA
Coppell, TX
12 October 2020

39735339R00085